CONTENTS

D1450454

Experiments

My friends and I like to play with water. We do a lot of fun things with it.

OUR WATER EXPERIMENT

Ethan Danielson

New York

Published in 2013 by The Rosen Publishing Group, Inc.
29 East 21st Street, New York, NY 10010

Book Design: Michael Harmon

Photo Credits: Cover © iStockphoto.com/Jaroslav74; p. 4 Jack Hollingsworth/Thinkstock.com; p. 5 michaeljung/
Shutterstock.com; p. 6 Michael Rolands/Shutterstock.com; p. 7 grynold/Shutterstock.com; p. 8 ARENA Creative/
Shutterstock.com; p. 9 Evgeny Karandaev/Shutterstock.com; p. 10 Dmitri Mihhailov/Shutterstock.com;
pp. 11, 14, 15 iStockphoto/Thinkstock.com; p. 12 Digital Vision./Thinkstock.com; p. 13 John Churchman/Photolibrary/Getty
Images; p. 16 Hemera/Thinkstock.com; p. 17 silver-john/Shutterstock.com; p. 18 Comstock/Thinkstock.com; p. 19 Don
Klumpp/The Image Bank/Getty Images; p. 20 PhotoAlto/Laurence Mouton/PhotoAlto Agency RF Collections/Getty Images;
p. 22 © iStockphoto.com/bmcent1.

ISBN: 978-1-4488-9031-6
6-pack ISBN: 978-1-4488-9032-3

Manufactured in the United States of America

CPSIA Compliance Information: Batch #WS12RC: For further information contact Rosen Publishing, New York, New York at 1-800-237-9932.

Word Count: 353

We like to swim. We like to play with water balloons.

We also like to do experiments.

An experiment is when you test or try something out.
It helps you find out new things. It's fun to experiment
with water.

Liquid

Water starts off as a **liquid**. A liquid is something that flows. You need a glass or other object to hold a liquid.

Freezing Water

In our first experiment, we made the water really cold.

This is called **freezing**. When we freeze water,

we make ice.

We froze water into small blocks called ice **cubes**.

An ice cube is a **solid**. The water took a long time

to freeze.

Our ice was hard. We held some in our hands. It made our hands feel cold!

We use ice for a lot of things. Ice keeps our food cold.

This lets us store food for a long time. Ice keeps our

drinks cold, too.

We also see ice outside. Snow is made of very little
pieces of ice. The snow makes everything feel cold.

Melting

Then we tried another experiment. We turned the ice back into water. This is called **melting**. Have you seen ice melt?

Melting happens when you make ice warm. We put the ice under a warm light. It melted into water. It made a puddle on the table!

The ice outside melts in the spring. It makes the ground wet. This gives Earth water to help our plants grow.

Steam

Next, we made the water really hot. Can you guess what happened? The water turned into **steam**!

Steam doesn't look like water, but it is. It rises
into the air because it's a gas. You can't hold it
in your hands.

Steam makes the air feel hot. Steam comes from a lot of different places. Taking a hot shower makes a lot of steam.

We tried one more experiment. We made the steam cool down. It turned back into water!

We saw drops of water on the lid of the pot.

The water wasn't hot anymore.

SOLID, LIQUID, GAS

solid	hard, does not flow, can be any size, can hold it
liquid	flows in your hand, need something to hold it, can be hot or cold
gas	light, cannot hold it, rises into the air, hard to see

We learned a lot through our experiments.

What experiments do you like to do?

GLOSSARY

cube (KYOOB) A solid with six sides.

freeze (FREEZ) To be made into ice by cold.

liquid (LIH-kwuhd) Something that flows like water.

melt (MEHLT) To change a solid to a liquid.

solid (SAH-luhd) Something that has its own shape and can be held in the hand.

steam (STEEM) Very hot water in the form of a gas.

INDEX